Flipping Houses

This book includes 2 manuscripts

Comprehensive Beginner's Guide for Newbies

The Cardinal Rules for Success

Table of Contents

Flipping Houses

Comprehensive Beginner's Guide for Newbies

Introduction

I want to thank you and congratulate you for ordering the book "Flipping Houses (Comprehensive Beginner's Guide for Newbies)."

This book has proven steps and strategies on how to become a truly accomplished flipper. You'll want to take advantage of these tips and strategies instead of heading into your first flip "blind," especially if you're entering into this business in hopes of making money. There are definitely some things you'll want to know and understand in this regard.

With this in mind, here's an inescapable fact: You will need this book to guide you through the flipping process, especially your very first flip. There are many things you need to know, from the first step of buying your first property, through rehabbing it and finally selling it. Everything you need to know is right here for you.

If you do not develop your flipping plan, you won't make millions. As such, we've outlined the steps to every part of your flip. From investing in a property to rehabbing it, and finally selling it for a profit. Everything you need to know is right here in this book for you.

Additionally, the art of Flipping Houses is only one component of the multi-faceted approach that falls under the broad spectrum of Real Estate Investing. Our books tackle all these other components in detail as well. To name just a few other topics that a successful Real Estate Investor should strive to understand, we have Rental Property Investing, Real Estate Sales with details on how to embark on a career as a successful Real Estate Agent, and even a step by step guide to achieving an excellent Credit Score to get you the loan with the best rates. And for anyone interested in the Tiny House Movement, we have books on that subject as well!!

You can find books on all of these topics- AND MORE- by visiting our Amazon Author Page at the following link: https://www.amazon.com/-/e/B01LYIFPLO

While this guide to Flipping Houses will provide a detailed technical analysis of the science behind the Flip, our other books will focus much more in depth on Real Estate Investing in general. If you check out our Real Estate Library, you are guaranteed to profit from Real Estate, Rental Properties, Flipping Houses, and turn this into a lucrative income stream for the rest of your life. Don't miss out!!

With all that being said, let's dive into the meat and potatoes of this book. It's time for you to become an amazing flipper.

Chapter 1
Understanding What House Flipping Is

Flipping: The act of buying a house then reselling it for a profit.

Although today's real estate market is still somewhat depressed, there's big money found in flipping houses. This is nothing more than simple economics: Buy low, sell high. You're sole intent is to buy a house and turn a profit with the highest rate possible and as fast as possible. In other words, you should never look at this as a long-term investment.

Unfortunately, you can't guarantee you'll see a profit when you flip a house because quite often you don't know what lies behind the walls until you actually buy the house. However, there are some things you can do to pad yourself along the way:

- Make sure you have liquid capital available for when something unforeseen happens.

- By keeping your day job you'll have stability and won't overstep your financial boundaries.

- Make sure you check out the deal for yourself. Don't pay for anything you haven't seen in person.

- Don't be lured in by the idea of fast cash.

- Never take on too much property at once because this will over extend your financial position, which is something you don't want to do.

There are various strategies used in flipping houses today. Each has its own advantages and disadvantages, giving you the opportunity to earn some extra money and the opportunity to build a profitable, long-term business.

Deciding if Flipping is for You: The pros and Cons

Not to scare you, but you really need to look at the pros and cons of flipping before you enter into this business. It's important you understand that while this is an easy, glamorous way of investing money and building wealth, there's still risk involved and you need to know that entering into this process.

With this in mind, let's first look at the cons, which include:

- The "Bubble Burst" is when there's a drop in real estate prices either at the national or local level. Typically, a higher supply than there is demand for housing causes this to occur. There are several reasons for this including increasing interest rates, increased lending rules, or local developers over-building in an area. New, extreme tax increases, and increasing crime rates often cause sudden drops in the value of real estate, making houses difficult or impossible to sell.

- You're always faced with the potential of losing money. While flipping is oftentimes a very profitable, short-term investment, if you don't properly budget your money and make room for both accounting mistakes and time delays, you could make a lot less money than you'd expected, break even, or lose money.

- It's also possible for you to over commit yourself. In the beginning, you'll probably think you can do more of the work yourself than is actually possible. Be realistic about the entire process or you'll seriously impair your budget and the overall project too. Often, this is the difference between making and losing money on a flip.

Now for the positive side of things, the pros include:

- There aren't many investments that will give you a crash course in budgeting faster than flipping will. You must learn to budget quickly if you want to profit from your flip. Otherwise, you'll watch yourself losing your profit. Here you mustn't only create a budget, but you have to stick to it. This is a vital skill for any successful flipper. Of course, this will also help you with your finances in other areas of your life as well.

- You'll greatly benefit from learning how to pay attention to details. This is a skill that will grow with each flip you do. It's important because you make or break your profit in your flip's small details. Potential buyers look for these things because it shows you care for your property.

- Watch as your credit rating grows exponentially. This will make it easier for you to borrow money in the future since banks look at loans you take out and pay back. By profiting on a flip, the bank grows more willing to lend you more money (a.k.a. increase your borrowing power) for your next flip. This is why if you can only start small, you should still get started and grow from there.

- The better you are at adapting to changes, the more successful you'll be at flipping houses. This is important because in business things change fast, even overnight. When these changes hit, it's important for you to change or update your business strategy so your success continues. This is also true with the techniques you learn along the way for rehabbing houses because what works for one house may not work for the next house.

Successfully flipping a house has the potential for a high yield investment. This can happen in a relatively short amount of time too. Of course, as with any high yield investment, flipping isn't without its risks. Therefore, you must carefully weigh both the pros and cons before you get involved with house flipping.

Types of Flipping

Essentially, there are two types of flipping:

- Wholesaling is when you buy a property and immediately resell it for a profit. You don't do any major repair or maintenance so you don't put up any money for the house. It's important you're a strong negotiator or this won't work. You must convince a seller to sell their property at well-below market value then convince the buyer to pay you near market value money.

- Rehabbing is when you buy property that's in disrepair, fix it up, then sell it. You can choose to focus on houses that need some minor repairs or tackle larger projects (e.g. houses with structural problems, fire damage, water damage).

The Cost of Flipping

One of the biggest questions on most people's minds is, "How much am I earn flipping houses?" There aren't any correct answers here since part-time flippers won't make as much as part-time flippers. Additionally, where you live plays a big role in how much a house sells for. However, if you manage one or two flips per month on your own you could average $40,000. So, over the course of a year, you could average between $240K and $480K. Obviously, the more flips you handle each month, the more money you'll make.

Taxes

Don't forget you have to pay taxes on your profits, though. "Profits" are defined as any money left from when you sell a house, minus your rehab costs (including labor and materials) and your fixed costs (e.g. commissions, fees, closing costs, loans, taxes, insurance, utilities). You're taxed at the same percentage as if you worked a full-time job. As such, they significantly eat into your profit margin. Once you're sure you're serious about flipping, make sure you consult a CPA who can help you structure your business so you pay the least amount of taxes possible.

8 Things you Must Know Before Starting Your First Flip

So, you think you're ready to get started with your first house flip? Well, before you do so it's important that you "know what you're doing." There are ways in which you can avoid losing money or spending too much of it when you're completing your first flip. With this in mind, here are the top 8 things you really should know before flipping your first house:

- Make sure you actually know what you're doing. You can't jump into the house flipping business blindly. While you don't need real estate experience to flip a house, you do need to make sure you maximize the time and money you invest into this business. Some of the things you must know include how to find funding; how to find, negotiate and close a great deal; what materials are popular; what high price items you should invest in; what low-cost materials you can use; how to hire inexpensive contractors; how to manage contractors, ensuring they meet your timeline; how to market your property properly; how to make the highest profit.

- Learn how to analyze a real estate deal. One of the biggest mistakes first-time flippers make is during this step. It's not easy to create a really sound investment. This is something you'll learn throughout your first deal.

- Never fudge your repair costs even if you're optimistic. When you have a complete inspection in the beginning, you may think you can make your budget really tight, but you never know when unforeseen issues may pop up. Even the most highly experienced flipper will tell you that you can never project too high of repair costs. As such, it's important you take a rational look at your repair costs.

- Never grow emotionally attached to your flip. Extravagance has no room here. You're working for profit. As such, you should only spend money on things that make sense, not the things you'd want if you were moving into the house (because you're not). It's important your choices are data driven. This is something you must thoroughly understand before starting your flip.

- Don't rationalize things. Stick to your original ARV. While temptation will arise, you shouldn't give into it ever. You also can't count on the market consistently appreciating. When a shift occurs, if you ignore your original ARV, you'll eliminate any room you had for profit.

- The faster you finish your flip and sell your house, the faster you pay back your loan and earn your profit to invest in your next flip. Things like hiring contractors, getting them to finish your project on time and selling your house are the most time-consuming aspects of your flip. This is why it's so important for you to know how to manage the project from the beginning to the end. Make sure you're comfortable negotiating and managing projects. These things play a vital role in making sure you earn the amount of money you want.

- It's important you know what's selling in your flip's neighborhood and why. You also need to know what buyers are expecting from those houses, as well as what's trending. The best way of accomplishing this is through online research and slowly driving through the neighborhood, looking at the other houses there.

- Never leave your contractors unsupervised. You also can't simply trust they're giving you reasonable prices. Instead, you must check on your contractors regularly and know what you should expect them to charge you for their time and materials. When contractors are unscrupulous they not only prolong the time it takes for you to sell the home, but they also cut into your profit margin because you'll have to pay more interest and take longer between flips. For these reasons, you must learn how to supervise and manage your contractors, keeping them on your timeline, not theirs.

While being an expert isn't necessary for you to start flipping houses, you do need to keep these things in mind. Throughout your firs flip you'll feel a mix of stress and excitement. It's during this time you'll learn enough to feel comfortable and confident with your next flip. Remember, knowledge is power and with the help of this book, there's no reason you can't have a successful first flip.

Chapter 2
Financing

Before you can flip a house, you must own the property first. This is where you'll need good credit so you can qualify for one of the following types of real estate financing. However, if you don't have good credit now, don't worry: There are still some ways you can buy your first property and enter the flipping business.

Conventional Financing

A mortgage broker or a large banking institution does this. They base your ability to qualify for a loan strictly on your current financial situation (e.g. credit score, income, assets, debt). Without good credit, reasonable income, and a low amount of debt, you probably won't qualify for this type of financing, but don't feel bad since most people won't qualify for it either.

While lenders offer low-interest rates, low loan costs, and a long loan duration for conventional financing, it's difficult to get because investors don't lend against properties that aren't move-in ready. For this reason, most lenders take a long time to appraise a house (usually 21 days) and if they're financing through Freddie Mac or Fannie Mae, which most do, you're limited to 4 – 10 loans at one time.

Portfolio/Investor Loans

Small banks (ones with only 3 – 5 branches) lend their own money, hence they're known as "portfolio lenders." As such, they choose who they want to loan to, but your financial situation doesn't matter as long as you don't have a bankruptcy, foreclosure, or any large unpaid debts on your credit. They'll take your real estate experience and the type of deal you're seeking into consideration, though. With this said, if they feel you have a solid investment, you'll more than likely receive financing.

Typically, you must put down less than 30% down payment with these loans. Some of these will even offer you a "rehab loan," meaning they roll the rehab costs into your loan. In either case, they're mostly concerned in making sure you're about to make a sound investment. Since they're highly accustomed to doing this, they can usually close your loan in 7 – 10 days.

Most portfolio loans are short-term (6 – 12 months), so it's important you're confident so you can finish the property and sell it in that amount of time. However, considering these loans usually have higher interest rates, it's in your best interest to complete the loan as soon as possible anyway. Also, remember the lender is very interested in your deal and will seriously scrutinize it. This is why they'll usually want to see that you have real estate experience.

Private Investors

These are well-off professionals (e.g. doctors, lawyers, business professionals) who have money (cash or retirement funds) to invest who expect better returns than what they'd receive from the stock market or other such venues, usually by about 8 - 12%. Usually, you already know these people so you can approach them easily.

This is great if you can prove your ability to find and execute real estate deals, these investors typically don't care about your creditworthiness. However, it can take a lot of work to convince these people to trust you with their money because they usually don't have much experience with real estate. This is why you need a good business plan, a track record of being a hard worker, and trustworthiness.

Hard Money Lenders

A hard money-lender (a.k.a. HML) loans against the property's value instead of against you, the borrower. Typically, they pool funds from wealthy people then lend the money to you at a high rate. These are good loans for new investors with little cash or experience because you can get them quickly.

While these loans are available, regardless of your financial situation, there are some definite drawbacks. For instance, they'll often charge you a higher lending rate. You must consider whether the money is worth the charges, but there are times when a HML will lend you 100% of both the purchase and rehab costs. However, considering the interest rates, which are usually 15% or more, this can eat up your profit margin rather quickly.

Equity Investors

These lenders will lend you money in return for a fixed percentage of the investment and the profit. They're more commonly known as a "partner with cash" because while you do all the work, ultimately you split the profit and only receive 50% of it as they take the other 50%. The nice thing is there are no "requirements" for you to fulfill so you can receive a loan since you're usually working with a friend or family member.

Besides the fact the lender takes 50% of your profit, another drawback to working with an equity investor is they typically want to take an active role in your investment. This is good only if they're experienced and share in your vision. Otherwise, it's usually a recipe for disaster.

Choosing the Right Type of Financing

When you're ready to check on which of these investors is a good fit for you, prepare yourself to have the following 5 key components of your financial resume scrutinized:

- Make sure you know your credit history and score. These numbers are important for getting your deals funded. You want a score of at least 680 or you'll find yourself immediately dismissed from consideration.

- Assets such as cash in the bank, stocks, bonds, large retirement accounts, property ownership, and investment properties all make your lender feel more comfortable working with you. This is because these things are usable when it's time to collateralize against your loan. However, be aware that if you can't repay your loan, the lender gets your collateral.

- Large amounts of debt make it difficult for you to get financing because lenders feel it will impede upon your ability to repay your loan. However, if you have a lot of debt (e.g. rent/mortgage, monthly bills, etc.) in comparison to your income, then you have a better chance of getting a loan with a low-interest rate (ideally, under 30%).

- Large amounts of debt make it difficult for you to get financing because lenders feel it will impede upon your ability to repay your loan. However, if you have a lot of debt (e.g. rent/mortgage, monthly bills, etc.) in comparison to your income, then you have a better chance of getting a loan with a low-interest rate (ideally, under 30%).

- Investing experience is also of concern to some lenders because those with a long investment history are much less of a risk than inexperienced investors. If you're inexperienced, a good business plan is sometimes a good substitute as it shows you have a well thought out plan and clear direction.

Flipping When You Have no Money

If you're like most aspiring investors today, you don't have any cash, credit, or money. This isn't something that should stop you, though. Instead, spend some time searching for another investor to partner with or either a HML or private lender.

When you do find someone who is willing to lend you money, it's important you know these tips for successful borrowing:

- They'll look at your credit score to decide if you're credit worthy. This is why you shouldn't borrow too much money and always repay what you owe on time.

- Make sure you understand the interest rate (the amount you're charged for borrowing money) and the loan's terms. Look for things like statements saying they'll charge you a penalty rate for prepaying your loan or there are late fees if your loan isn't paid by a certain time each month.

- Think carefully about how much money you borrow. Since you're charged an interest rate, you'll ultimately end up paying back more money. This is why you don't want to borrow more money than you need or can afford.

- The application process requires you give your lender various types of information (e.g. credit score, proof of income). You'll want to know what information to take with you when you're applying for a loan, especially if you need the money immediately.

- Know what the repayment period (how long you have to repay your loan) is. The shorter the repayment period, the less interest you'll pay, but this also requires you pay slightly more on your loan.

- Have a plan for repaying the loan before borrowing the money.

Chapter 3
Finding a Property

Knowing how to borrow money is important. Armed with that knowledge and ability, you'll want to start looking at houses. One of the most common ways of doing this is by finding a Realtor, but a few other methods exist and are worth mentioning as well.

Budgeting for Your First Flip

Decisions you make about the house you're flipping, either before or during the project, can and will affect the size of your profit. This is why it's so important you create a budget for your whole project, not just the purchasing and rehabbing prices, and then stick to it.

With this in mind, here's a checklist you can use while creating the budget for your first flip:

- You must start by determining the after repair value (ARV) of your flip. This is what you can base your expected ROI upon once you've placed the house on the market. A trusted Realtor will help you choose your property's estimated ARV.

- Rehab costs vary greatly depending on the house you buy and how much rehab work it needs. Make sure you track all the house's necessary repairs. This will make you much more knowledgeable when it comes time for your next flip.

- Financing and carrying costs are easy to overlook, but make sure you don't. These costs include your loan, as well as paying for things until you sell the house. Some of the items you can't afford to overlook and which fall into this category include financing loan(s), property taxes, utilities (e.g. gas, water, electric), property insurance, and sometimes you'll also need to pay HOA or condo fees. You should also note that the longer your rehab work takes, as well as the amount of time your post-rehab house remains on the market, the higher your carrying costs will be. This will diminish your flip's profit too.

- Realtor fees are also involved because while you can sell your flip yourself if you want the fastest turnaround time on your investment and the biggest profit, you should hire a good real estate agent. Not only are they worth their commission fee, but they'll also help you save money on your flip in the long run.

- Some of the other costs that often get overlooked include inspection fees, interest on loans, contingencies, and closing costs.

Typically, you can break your average budget down into the following cost percentages:

- 53.25% of your budget will go towards the house's buying price

- 20% of your budget will pay for labor

- 6.5% of your budget will pay for materials

- 8% of your budget will pay for carrying costs, utilities, commissions, and other hidden fees

- 12.25% will result in profit

Realistic budgeting is the key to reduced risk. Of course, there's nothing that will cut the inherent risks associated with house flipping, but creating a realistic budget will most definitely help mitigate at least some of your risk. Another way in which you can "manage" some of these risks is by becoming as thoroughly knowledgeable in the realm of house flipping as you can before making your first investment. Also, make sure you always follow the old saying, "Never invest more than you can afford to lose."

Finding a Realtor

Since you don't want just any Realtor, there are some things you'll want to do so you learn more about this person before hiring them:

- Talk with clients to find out what the Realtor's asking price is, what type of house they, how long their house was on the market, and how they felt about their experience.

- Contact the state licensing board to see if they're in good standing.

- Find out if they've ever won the "Realtor of the Year" award by the state or local branch of the National Association of Realtors (NAR). These are Realtors whose peers voted them "the best."

- Check out their credentials and specialties (what areas they have special training in). There are many of these credentials, including CRS (Certified Residential

Specialist) completed training in handling residential real estate; ABR (Accredited Buyer's Representative) completed training buyer representation, and SRES (Seniors Real Estate Specialist) completed training in helping senior citizens.

- Learn how long the agent has been in business. You want someone with over 5 years experience and who specializes in the neighborhood and price range your flip is in.

- Review their current listings. Make sure they're effectively using the Internet since this is where most people begin their search. This is another opportunity for you to see if they're selling properties like yours. It's also important the Realtor has plenty of listings without having so many you become just a number to them.

- Find out what other houses are for sale near yours. Your Realtor should be able to tell you about them without having to look the information up. If they have to go searching for the information, they don't really know their properties.

Finding a Realtor with these qualifications may take some work, but it's well worth it. With them by your side, it's time to find your first house to flip. You'll need to put some thought into this as well. Although you don't plan on living here, this is still important because it affects your investment's value.

The Importance of Your Flip's Location

Understanding your location's importance, here's what you should think about:

- Geographic location: What part of the country do you want to flip houses in? Things like house prices, job opportunities, and good schools are important.

- City vs. suburbs vs. rural: What setting is best? Here you must consider how much peace and quiet is important, how big of lot size you need, and how close you want your property located to things people want and need.

- Neighborhood: What characteristics are important to you here? You'll want a place where people feel comfortable, have good schools, and stores nearby. People will pay more to live in a good neighborhood with good schools and where the overall neighborhood is safe so they don't continually need to watch their backs.

- You should also visit the property during the day and again at night. Neighborhoods don't typically appear the same on paper as they do when you're in them. Little details (e.g. narrow streets, cars parked on the street) often make a huge difference. It's also important to understand neighborhoods may feel comfortable throughout the day then feel disconcerting at night. The same is true of neighborhoods during different types of weather.

Once you know what factors are most important to you about location, you need to research some neighborhoods, especially if you're not already familiar with these locations. You can easily find all kinds of facts and statistics online. However, it's also a good idea to talk to the neighborhood's current residents and local police department to get more information.

All of these things clearly affect your flip's renovation potential. Another important thing that influences this is how much work the house really needs and whether you can do it. According to Jeff Beneke, author of "The Fence Bible," you want to make sure it's possible to close off one part of a house at a time when you're turning it into an apartment building. This allows you to "close off one room at a time, do what you have to do in that, move somebody into there, then close off another room" and keep working.

Buying Your First Flip

When you find jobs you don't feel comfortable doing yourself, it's important to get estimates on the cost of that work before buying the property. If the cost of this work places the house at a higher value than others in the neighborhood, it's not a good investment unless you can somehow scale back the other renovations.

While it's important to "pretend you're living there," you shouldn't allow these pretty, clean properties to romance you. This isn't what you're getting into. Instead, take a few moments to:

- Try everything in the house (e.g. flush the toilets, turn on the lights, climb the stairs, check the water flow in the showers and sinks)

- Look up at the ceiling instead of only looking at floors and walls because then you'll know if there's any water damage.

Think Long-Term

You'll want to keep these things in mind as you look at the various types of properties available for you to buy today. They include:

- Distressed properties are houses whose owners aren't maintaining and thus they're either neglected or in poor condition. The price of such houses is usually well below market value, making them very interesting to many flippers. However, the main risk is the house's condition.

- Commercial property includes stores, offices, warehouses, hotels, malls, farms, apartment buildings, and garages. These have income potential so typically you'll see a 6 – 12% annual return off your buying price. At the same time, you'll also receive a more objective price evaluation. However, these properties take a lot of time, regardless how many tenants or business owners occupy the property. As such, you'll need professional help with these types of properties, right from the beginning since they need a larger initial investment too. This makes everything much riskier.

- Foreclosed properties are ones in which the lender is trying to recover the loan's balance from a borrower who's stopped making payments. This often allows you to buy a better house or one in a better neighborhood. It's also financially advantageous since you pay less than market value. Unfortunately, these houses are typically overdue for house repairs including mold buildup, broken pipes, vermin, and bug infestations.

Finding the Best Deal

Regardless what type of property you choose to buy, you should always watch for the best deal. Some ways of finding these deals include:

- Drive around a neighborhood you like and find a house you think needs some work. Once you find a distressed or vacant property, write down its address and any notes, even a few photos. With this house dig into the public records or do a reverse phone number search, then write a letter offering to buy the property.

- Send out direct mail (a large number of targeted letters or postcards) to people who may want to sell their house. This sometimes seems like shooting in the dark, but if you send out 1,000 letters and 5% of the recipients (50 people) call for more information, then 5% of these folks sell you their house, you'll buy 2 houses. As such, this is actually money well spent.

- Target landlords going through evictions because this is a stressful, expensive time that makes many of them question whether they want to continue in this business. You can find them by looking through your county's public record.

- Conduct an online search. Look through various forums and on Craigs List. In doing so, you'll want to search for sellers, post ads, and search for landlords. When searching for landlords, you want to avoid professional property management companies. Instead, call up the other landlords, explain you want to invest in real estate in that area and wondered if they'd consider selling you their property. Even if they don't want to sell their property, they probably know someone who wants to sell theirs.

- Get deals from wholesalers, which are people who find great deals on real estate, contract them, then sell them to another investor for slightly more money. Make sure you only work with good ones or consider training someone to do this work for you.

Your House's Contract

After you use one of these methods to find a property to buy, you're on to the contract. It's essential you understand the contract and that it meets your expectations. Typically, the language used in it is relatively easy to understand.

Nonetheless, you must still move forward with caution since it's legally binding and misinterpretation can cost a lot of money.

With this in mind, make sure you:

- Consult a real estate dictionary so you can understand any unfamiliar terms.

- Read the contract thoroughly, checking for accuracy about the property's location, price, down payment, financing, closing date, and contingencies.

- See the seller's responsibilities clear defined.

- Have a warranty clause obligating the seller to give you a clear title.

- Verify the contract's details, which should include what happens to your good-faith deposit if the transaction isn't completed, as well as provisions for an inspection and a final walk-through before closing.

- Carefully note the precise conditions for contract withdrawal terms.

- Talk to a real estate attorney if anything isn't clear. While this costs a fee, it's important you make sure everything is clear before signing a contract.

Chapter 4
The Work Itself

While a range of 20 – 30% of a house's value is an acceptable amount to invest in renovations, this is only true when you plan on living there for 10 or more years. Since you're flipping the house, you really only should invest 15 – 20% of its value in its remodel.

Over Rehabbing and Under Rehabbing

It's important to understand you can also over or under rehab a property. You must keep things reasonable, especially if you're dealing with distressed properties, under market value. Aim for buying a house at 20% under market value, doing some light rehab then reselling it for a 12% annual return on investment (ROI). Of course, the level of rehab depends on the house's location. Overdoing a rehab causes your ROI to plummet. Of course, not doing enough rehab, especially in a really nice neighborhood, means the house will sit and sit.

Choosing What to Rehab

To decide what to repair on a house, look at the other houses in the neighborhood. Look at what materials they used and their quality. Typically, the more expensive a neighborhood, the better you should make your rehab.

While you're not using your money on the flip, you must pay back any money you've borrowed so you don't want to over borrow. Regardless what you pay up front, the most important number is your after repair value (ARV). You can figure this out by knowing what you can sell the property for when you're finished flipping it. Do this by accessing the MLS, which allows you to compare the other houses like yours that sold in the past 6 months. If no other houses have sold, there may be no demand for the type of house you're selling. Also, look at what Realtors priced these houses at. With this number in mind, you can start deciding what you should pay for the various costs associated with your flip.

Knowing When to Stop

After spending some time flipping houses you'll eventually run into one that's a total flop. Regardless how much research you did on the property and its neighborhood, along with the time you invested in finding great deals, you'll still run across a few of these types of houses.

How do you know when you've reached the point where you simply can't do anything more for a house? There are four ways you'll know when it's time to stop. They include:

- Take a look at what the house needs in comparison to your rehab budget. While some houses look great from the outside, you'll find structural damage or leaky ceilings when you go inside. Things like this threaten to take up your entire rehab budget and turn what looks like a great flip into a major nightmare. This is when you need to step back and decide how much work you can do and how much work you need the professionals to do for you. Thinking this through will help you shave some money off so you stay in your budget. However, don't waste a lot of time here because you're losing money. So, if you think the professionals can do the work better and faster, you probably should just let them go ahead and do the work for you.

- Don't get involved with a flip that needs structural repairs unless you have "deep pockets." This is why your contractors should take a really good look at the entire house before you start doing anything. Structural damage will quickly eat up your whole budget so instead of investing all your money in this, step back and consider what you'll need to do to get the house in living condition. If that's not possible, then you'll have to consider demolishing the entire house and starting all over again.

- Put your rehab tasks in order of importance. Make the house's exterior first on your list so you can get a "for sale" sign up on it fast. For this, you need to make the home look good because curb appeal makes the first, and most vital, impression. Of course, you don't want to start showing your house while contractors are still working on it. This generates interest in the home while you're working on it. You can then use this interest to gauge how much work you can afford to do.

- Remember the main principle of flipping is getting the house in the best shape possible for its market so you can make a really good profit for yourself. Now, this doesn't mean you should do poor quality work, but this principle should help guide you as you decide what you need to do to bring the home up to market value and sell it as quickly as possible.

They call this process "flipping" for a reason. It's because the sooner you get the house into great shape while remaining within your budget, the sooner you'll see a return on your investment and be ready to move on to your next flip. So, if a little detail here or there isn't going to do anything to improve the house's value, then don't do it. It's time to sell the house instead.

Don't Overlook Financing Costs

Here you need to ask your Realtor how long other houses in your neighborhood have sat on the market. Your Realtor should also be able to give you his thoughts on why some houses are selling while others aren't. It's important you only borrow as much money as you need for buying and flipping the house, but don't forget you also have other bills to pay along the way too (e.g. electric bill, gas bill, water bill, insurance, lawn mowing, property taxes).

When you break this down to numbers, it may look something like this:

- You get a $120,000 loan at 10% interest meaning your annual interest is $12,000 ($120,000 x 10% = $12,000)

- You spend four months renovating the house, which then sits on the market for a month and closing takes a month so you pay 6 months of interest or $6,000

Obviously, your biggest cost is the renovation itself, especially since you don't want to get involved in unethical "fix and flips." Instead, you want to do high-quality work while maintaining healthy profit margins. Of course, you don't have to do any of this work yourself. There are many different types of contractors available for you to choose from today, including:

- A really good handyman can tackle many of the different parts of your rehab for you (e.g. carpentry, sheet-rock, basic electrical, basic plumbing, basic HVAC).

- A general contractor is basically a licensed handyman, but he can also hire and pay subcontractors. This allows him to have more time for handling scheduling and the budget.

- Contractors are different from a general contractor. If you choose to use them without hiring a general contractor, it's important you're much more hands on in scheduling and managing them. The county you live in licenses and insures contractors in the area they specialize in. Some of the most well-known contractors include Terminex (pest/termite) and Roto Rooter (plumbing).

Your goal is to have these people in place the day you close on the property so you can start working right away. This is also the day you want all the utilities switched over into your name and turned on. The project's success relies on you, ultimately. As such, you have to keep on top of everything. Ask questions, know what's going on at all times, and visit the job site as often as possible to keep everything on schedule.

When using a general contractor, make sure to outline how and when you'll distribute all the draws (a payment made to the contractor for work that's been completed). There are some guidelines you should follow here:

- The first draw should happen at the beginning of the project before starting any work. With this draw, your contractor can buy the necessary materials for starting the work. Make sure this isn't more than 25% of the project's total cost, though.

- Make more draws at agreed upon "milestones" (when they've completed specific jobs).

- At the end of the flip, make sure you're happy with everything before making the last draw.

Sometimes extra or unexpected issues arise costing you money. If you're not careful, this can really blow your budget and eat away at your ROI. While you should expect things to come up, make sure you're in control of approving them before they spend any money. This way you can carefully check it instead of just agreeing because the contractor said so. It's your job to ask questions so you truly understand what they're spending the money on.

Always remember, this is your project, you are in control. This is why being on premises regularly is so important. However, you should remember that you're not there to work or run errands for anyone. It's your contractor's job to manage the project, get the materials, and coordinate the subcontractors. You're there to look at the work's quality as it's done so you can point out any issues as soon as you see them. In doing so you'll feel more comfortable tactfully pointing out things that you must fix, instead of presenting your contractor with a long list of items. Of course, this also makes your general contractor more aware that you're on top of things and that you actually pay attention to details. In turn, this will make him more conscious of the details as well.

Chapter 5
Selling Your Flip

Since you've already managed all the house flipping work, you may think you can now manage the sale of the house yourself as well. However, you should know that the money you'd spend on commissions is typically a wash when you consider the cost of hiring an experienced Realtor. This is because most houses that are "for sale by owner" (FSBO) take longer to sell and then when they do sell, they typically sell for less money.

Reasons to Hire a Realtor

If the money wasn't enough of an incentive for hiring a Realtor, here are some other really good reasons for doing so:

- This is a major business transaction which includes three important negotiations along the way: the initial offer, followed by the counter offer, then once everyone reaches an agreement, there's the post-offer (e.g. inspections, requests for concessions).

- It's important your house receive as much exposure as possible in front of lots of potential buyers. Your Realtor prepares all the marketing.

- materials, coordinates the online marketing, hosts open houses, and networks with other agents who have potential buyers.

- A Realtor typically represents most buyers. They're usually deterred by an FSBO because they're afraid the won't receive their commission.

- The process is smoother because Realtors know how to efficiently work their way through the sales process.

For Sale by Owner

Of course, if you're dead set on selling the house yourself, you should know there are some benefits to doing this as well. They include:

- You pay yourself instead of paying an agent commission.

- Since your house probably doesn't have much equity, you may end up paying some of the Realtor's commission yourself. You can avoid this with a FSBO and thus you'll lose money.

- You'll still have work to do when you work with a Realtor (e.g. repairs, cleaning, staging). Then when you do find a buyer the two of you will need to figure out how to pay the Realtor's commission. So, while a FSBO is a lot of work, you'll receive a great payout for doing so, especially considering you won't lose money in any of these ways.

- When you do have a FSBO you'll have expenses like the cost of an appraisal, running ads in your local newspaper, and hiring a lawyer to oversee the contract. However, you're in control of these things yourself with a FSBO. You'll also want to learn how to stage your house since you won't have anyone to do it for you.

Staging Your Flip for a Faster Sale

Staging is the act of preparing your house for sale. Your goal is to make your house look truly appealing to most people so you can quickly sell it for more money. You also want to help your potential buyer envision themselves living in the house. With this in mind, here are some things you should do:

- Arrange each room to showcase its purpose.

- Make sure the rooms are all painted in neutral colors.

- Scrub the floors.

- Deodorize the house so there are no nasty smells.

- Bake fresh-baked cookies to serve or boil cinnamon sticks on the stove before each showing.

- Don't forget about enhancing curb appeal! Since this is the buyer's first impression, it's somewhat more important than cleaning the inside of the house. So, mow the lawn and pick up any trash.

Having Your Flip Appraised

All of these things will help with your house's appraisal as well. This is a professional's "educated guess" (opinion) of the size, condition, function and quality of your house. A credible financial institution won't lend a buyer money for a house until they've conducted an appraisal. This is because the bank wants to know what the loan collateral will sell for in a worst-case scenario," says Bart Jackson, an appraiser, and Realtor with Charleston Preferred Properties in Charleston, South

Carolina. They don't want stuck with a house they lent a buyer money for only to discover it's not worth its buying price.

This is how the appraisal process works... When they arrive on your property they will:

- Inspect your house

- Research the value of other houses in your neighborhood to see what they're selling at and arrive at a fair market value.

- Provide you with a final report which includes all their data and research, as well as their final "opinion of value."

Real estate attorney Robert Pellegrini from Bridgewater, Massachusetts issues a word of caution about this process in that if your appraisal comes in under purchase price, most buyers will have room in their contract to end or renegotiate the contract. This is why it's best for both parties to get this appraisal, but you, the seller, is the one who must pay for it at the time of closing. Typically, this will cost up to several hundreds of dollars.

Having Your Flip Appraised

This appraisal is different from your house inspection, which is also necessary. Inspectors usually arrive before appraisers and are there to look for any defects in the house that would cost the buyer money later on. Of course, if an appraiser notices a problem they will point it out to the inspector and vice versa.

The appraisal process typically takes a week or two. This is because underwriters can ask for more information and pictures of the house than in the past. There really isn't anything you can do to move this process along, but staging your house and having a list of all the repairs (nothing formal or detailed, just a list) you've done to it are both beneficial. If you have a Realtor, they'll meet the appraiser at the house to share this list, and any other pertinent information, with them. Your Realtor can also give the appraiser other information, including that on comparable houses to justify your house's selling price.

Having Your Flip Inspected

As stated before, the inspector arrives later in the process and is different from the appraiser. They're the ones who really take a close, deep look at your house to see if there are any "hidden" issues. You don't only want to hire one after you've rehabbed a house, but some people will encourage you to hire one before buying one too. This is because they can tell you a lot about the property's condition. Of course, you can also become really good at this job and do it yourself.

Some things a good inspector will look for include looking for:

- Any sign of mold, water leakages, cracks or leaks in the foundation, rotting wooden beams in the basement, as well as ensuring that the plumbing systems should also be in good working order

- Moisture and cracks in the crawl space, if one exists

- Evidence of water leakage or damage in the attic

- Sufficient insulation for your area of the country

- Leaks, water stains, and mildew, as well as water pressure and proper drainage in the bathroom and kitchen plumbing

- Easy access to the main breaker box or fuse box, that's in good condition

- A sufficient number of electrical outlets

- Ground fault circuit interrupters (a.k.a. GFCI) to prevent shock from occurring in both the kitchen and the bathroom

- An appropriately sized HVAC system

- Shingles - accounted for and in good condition

- Gutters and downspouts offer adequate water damage

- A good drainage system

- The foundation, making sure it doesn't have any drainage issues

- The ground sloping away from the foundation

- Driveways and walkways that are even and not cracking

- Siding that's in good repair

- Trees, shrubbery, and plants don't look overgrown or unkempt

- Sprinkler systems properly working

- Decks and porches aren't decaying nor do they have any termite damage

- Steps and railings are secure

- Fireplaces' and chimneys' mortar isn't loose and crumbling

- Ceilings, walls, and floors aren't leaking

- Drywall isn't pulling away from interior walls

- Walls and ceilings don't have any cracks

- Floors aren't spongy or weak nor do they lean

- Doors and windows move smoothly and close properly

- Windows don't have evidence of mildew, moisture, or fog

- The garage's flooring isn't stained or cracked

- The garage's siding is in good condition

- Garage doors work properly

- The garage's foundation drains properly

- Soil slopes away from the garage

There are many things to look at and think about when buying and selling a house. This is why you should have a house inspection. Once you have these results, you can decide if the property is worth buying or how much to sell your house for. If you receive a bad inspection, you're helpless when it comes to whether or not the buyer will back out. However, if you're the one buying the house, you can try to buy the house for a lower price.

Throughout this time you need to keep your head up. Even if you receive a bad review this may not throw the buyer off because most of them expect to have to do some work anyway. If not, you should at least be able to reach a compromise that works for everyone. On the other hand, if you're planning on flipping the house, simply get some quotes on the work you need to do. With multiple bids, you can see how much it will take and use this to your benefit during negotiations.

Closing the Deal

You'll need to head into closing with this head up, positive thinking, "We can negotiate this" type of attitude. After all, closing day is a celebratory day. This is just a formality composed of signing paperwork, exchanging money, and shaking hands. However, you need to do some preparatory work to make sure it goes this way.

According to New York real estate attorney Neil Garfinkel communication is the key to success when it comes time for closing. So, a week before closing, talk to the people who represent you.

Stay on your loan officer or agent to make sure they have everything they need, including loan papers. It's also important to understand that by law you're allowed to check the closing settlement statement or the HUD-1 form 24 hours before closing. Make sure you take advantage of this time to compare the form to your good faith estimate (a.k.a. GFE form) that you received when you applied for your loan.

Make sure you have everything you're going to sign before signing it. This way you don't grow nervous when you go to closing and it's simply a matter of signing the papers and getting the keys. Also, by looking over the loan documents beforehand, you'll know exactly what to take with you to the closing.

Some of the items you'll typically need include:

- A certified check is definitely needed. While using a wire transfer is an option, typically this takes longer instead of being faster. This is because the closing won't happen until they actually have the wire confirmed. Depending on this timing, you could have a major problem.

- A photo ID

- Copies of your insurance policy for the property

- The GFE form, HUD-1 statement, or both in the event there are discrepancies

Even with all this planning, you won't know for certain if everything will go as planned and you'll get out of there in less than 30 minutes or things will go awry and you'll need more time. This is why you don't want to try to do this business on your lunch hour. Keep in mind delays are more likely if you're closing near the end of the month.

You also never know what will happen at the closing table. Some of the biggest holdups include:

- Double checking the numbers on the mortgage only to discover inconsistencies (e.g. correcting the interest rate or amount)

- A simple typo means the loan documents need sent back to the lender so they can redo them

This is why you should try to schedule your closing for earlier in the day. Also, you should never wait to the last day on your contract for holding your closing, especially if you're buying a foreclosed property or a short sale.

Chapter 6
The Formula Behind Flipping

There are many strategies Realtors use today when selling houses. One of the most popular is the "99" strategy. This is when you sell your house for $499K instead of $500K. In doing so, the $1K you lose covers some of the buyer's closing costs, but the buyer thinks they're paying $500K. Ultimately this $1K doesn't mean much to you or the buyer, but there's a lot of strategy and psychology behind this.

Choosing Your Pricing Strategy

Ultimately, you need to listen carefully to your agent's pricing strategy because they know what will and what will not work. It's also important you understand that this isn't something you simply do then forget about. There are lots of factors you must consider, but you can't expect all of them, which is why you must stay flexible so you can quickly react to any change in market conditions or if you receive new information.

With this in mind, it's important to understand that there are four different types of pricing strategies you can use as a seller. These are:

- You don't want only one person interested in your house because real estate has some high stakes. If you price your house on the lower end of this range, you'll stimulate interest among several buyers. This works best if you're not in a big rush to sell the house.

- You want to make sure you know the price-point people typically search for when looking for a house in the neighborhood where your property is. This is important because if you list your house over that price-point and a Realtor creates and automated buyer search in their local database for properties under a set amount and you price your house slightly over that amount, it won't come up on their search. Unfortunately, this happens often.

- Never get "creative" with your asking price because this draws unnecessary attention to your house as if you'd painted the house purple. Buyers will want to know why you chose that figure, who the seller is, and so on. You want to stay as far in the background as possible, if not make yourself completely invisible. After all, your goal is to showcase your property and appeal to as many people as possible. If you get really quirky when it comes to your asking price, you'll contradict what is a "tried and true" strategy.

As you use one of these strategies and before you actually place your house on the market, make sure you work out a pricing contingency plan, especially if you want to try a higher price tag than you think you'll actually get. By having a "Plan B" you'll save yourself time and know what to expect if things don't work out with your original price tag.

The Importance of Considering Your Rehab Costs

You know you'll need to do a lot of work on your flip, but just how much is something you're probably wondering. When you've flipped a few houses, this is a number that's easier for you to know and understand (guessing repair costs within about 1 – 2% just from knowing the size and condition of the house) from the starting point, when you're just buying a house. However, if this is your first flip, there's a way of estimating the cost of your flip.

To estimate the cost of your repair costs, here are some helpful tips:

- Most houses in need of a "standard" cosmetic rehab will cost $20 per square foot. A "standard" rehab usually consists of all new flooring (carpet and tile or hardwood), paint (interior and exterior), baseboards, fixtures for both electric and plumbing, window treatments (blinds), doors, and some landscaping. So, if you buy a 1,500 sq. ft. house you'll spend around $30K on the rehab (1,500 x $20 = $30,000). Of course, if your house is a higher-end property, you'll need to spend $25 - $30 per square foot.

- Now adjust either up or down based on what else the house needs or what it doesn't need. For instance, if your house's kitchen is newly remodeled, you won't need to do anything more to it and you can remove the cost from your rehab costs. If you only need to repaint (interior and exterior) and redo the floors, you can do this for $2K - $5K. However, if you need to redo the roof, this typically costs $5K - $8K alone; a new HVAC system, $5K; new windows, $200 per window. Other things you may need to do include rewiring the electrical, redoing the plumbing, and structural requirements. Make sure you have this in mind when you come up with your first offer price, then when you have your offer accepted you and a licensed contractor can go through the property together to create a detailed "scope of work" and repair estimates just to make sure you didn't miss anything.

Estimating the Costs of Your Flip

One of this industry's biggest pitfalls comes from underestimating repair costs. Heed this warning! You're bound to come across unexpected repair costs when you flip a house, regardless how careful you are. This is because how much of the house you must fix can range from "almost nothing" to "almost everything.

With this checklist you can enter into a flip anticipating all the repair costs:

- The house itself: Does it need a simple cosmetic paint job? Do you need to change some fixtures? Do you need to gut the entire kitchen?

- The General Contractor: There's a good reason you want your general contractor involved from the start. Often, they know what you don't know about construction. Trying to do things without them will usually cost you more money than hiring them in the first place. You want a general contractor who knows what they're doing and will stick with your project until it's done.

- Subcontractors: These are the people who you'll turn to for specific repairs and fixes. They include painters, plumbers, and electricians. Your general contractor will help you get fair quotes from them, many general contractors will even find them for you.

- Carrying costs: Don't overlook these! You'll "own" the property for a few months. During that time you're responsible for the general upkeep of the property. This includes paying for utilities (e.g. gas, water, electric), insurance, and property taxes. Also, you may have to pay HOA or condo fees.

- Expecting the unexpected: Regardless of how careful you are, more than likely you'll come up with some surprises and their bill. You must always expect this to happen so you can build a buffer into the total amount you've estimated for repair costs. With this in mind, usually 10% over the number you've come up with is a good buffer.

Calculating Your Closing and Holding Expenses

When you watch house flipping shows, nobody ever seems to talk about closing and holding costs. You don't want all your profits sucked up in this way, so you do need to know about these things.

First, remember the closing costs. These are the buyer's closing costs, which are typically less than the selling closing costs. When you're buying a flip, you'll pay these costs. They're typically 0.5% of your purchasing price.

Secondly, don't forget sellers have closing costs too. These are the seller's closing costs and are somewhat more expensive than purchase closing costs. If you're using a Realtor, expect to pay them 5 – 6% commission. In certain areas and markets, your Realtor may also want you to pay for some of their expenses, which ranges from 1 – 6%, but typically is about 3%. So, make sure you include these percentages for closing costs.

Third, and finally, there are holding costs. Lots of people forget to think about these. However, you must still pay for things like property taxes, insurance, utilities, maintenance (e.g. lawn), and HOA while you "own" the house. Make sure you're aware of these expenses because depending on how long you hold on to the property, you'll have increased expenses.

Remembering Your Financing Costs

By now you're probably hoping there aren't any more expenses to think about. However, if you've used financing to buy your flip then you'll need to consider your financing costs. Obviously, this section doesn't apply to anyone who's using their own capital or have people they know financing the property.

Unfortunately, financing costs can really add up. Typically they work out to:

- A private money-lender: You'll pay between 8 – 12% annualized return on your capital.

- A hard money-lender: You'll pay a 12% annualized rate with extra (percentage) points and fees. Usually, your points are between 2 – 3 (2 – 3%) or about 1% per month you have the loan.

When you Don't Make Enough Money

Flipping houses is expensive. The expenses begin with acquiring the property. While there are lots people claiming low or no money financing, receiving these loans is difficult. So, if you must finance your acquisition, you must also pay interest. Don't forget this money is tax-deductible. However, this isn't a 100% deduction. So, every dollar you spend on interest adds to the amount of money you must earn when you sell the house so you break even on the deal.

Some people think by paying cash they'll get rid of the interest, but property holding costs still exist regardless of how you pay for the property itself. It's important you add these renovation costs into your closing price. When you plan to actually make a profit, you must make sure your sale price exceeds your cost of acquisition, cost of holding the property, and the cost of renovations combined.

Even if you manage to break even with these things, you still need to think about capital gains taxes. These still have a way of chipping away at your profit.

When you run out of Time

Renovating and flipping houses takes a lot of time. Initially, you spend months searching for the right property to buy. Once you own the house, you spend months rehabbing it before you can sell it. Don't forget during this time you must also schedule inspections to make sure the work you've done complies with the applicable building codes. If it doesn't, you'll need to spend more time and money to correct the issues. Then, finally, you'll need to invest more time into selling the property. If you choose to show your house yourself, this will take lots of time commuting and meeting with potential buyers.

Making a 10% profit on a $50K house results in a $5,000 profit. Some people think they're better off getting a good job whereby they'll earn this money in a few weeks or months from a steady paycheck without the time commitment and risk involved in flipping. This isn't meant to keep you from investing in flipping, but to make sure this is really what you want to do.

When you Don't Have Enough Skills or Knowledge

Professional builders, carpenters, and plumbers often flip houses on the side of their regular jobs because they have the knowledge, skills, and experience to find a house then fix it up and make some extra money. Of course, some of these people also work for unions that pay them an unemployment check throughout the winter months while they work on their flips. Regardless of how they do it, they understand that the real money made from house flipping is found in sweat equity. So, if you're good with a hammer, carpeting, hanging drywall, roofing, or install a kitchen sink, you have the necessary skills for flipping a house. However, if you have to pay a professional to do all this work for you, your profit margin will be dramatically reduced.

The same can also be said about knowledge because without it there's no way of choosing right property, in the right location, for the right price. Even if you get a great deal, you still need to know what renovations to make and which to forego. Regardless of the deal, there are also tax laws to understand and you also need to know when to cut your losses before your project turns into a money pit.

When you Don't Have Enough Patience

As a professional, you'll want to take your time and wait for the "perfect" property to avail itself to you. This is something most novices don't do, though. Instead, they rush out and buy the first property they see then hire the first contractor they find only to wonder why things are so expensive or take so long. Professionals don't run into this problem with contractors either because they pre-arrange them, ensuring they find ones who not only fit into their budget but also are reliable.

Once the house is ready for you to place it on the market for sale, you don't want to just hire any Realtor. This is what novices do, but as a professional, you'll want to at least give the FSBO model a good try. Doing so will lower your costs while maximizing your profits.

You can't rush through everything. It takes time for you to do everything. Unfortunately, sometimes your profit margin is slim while at other times you'll hit the jackpot.

Determining Sales Price and Your Profit

New investors typically want to know how much money they can make from flipping houses. This is because over the past decade many TV shows have shown flippers making great money. However, you should know that while some of these shows are realistic, others are somewhat contrived. Also, many of these shows give you the purchase price, rehab price, and the sales price. What they fail to show you are the other costs (e.g. closing costs, Realtor expenses, taxes, insurance, utilities, maintenance). You must consider those costs will you arrive at a realistic view of the profits.

It's also important to understand that you understand houses sell for different prices in different parts of the country. This pricing difference is also true about the various other expenses associated with rehabbing a house. Additionally, housing demand varies. The point here is the profit you make from flipping a house in Florida isn't the same as the profits you make from flipping a house in California nor will the cost of flipping a house in New Jersey be the same as the cost of flipping a house in Iowa.

You must also take into account other expenses as well, including taxes, insurance, utilities, and closing costs. These expenses vary depending on the state and even the house's neighborhood.

Additionally, it's interesting to note that in those areas where houses are lower priced, investors are more likely to pay for them in cash instead of taking out a loan. This makes sense when you think about the cost of financing, though. When you use cash to buy a house, you can maximize the flip's potential profit market since you won't have to pay any financing fees.

Setting up Your First Flip

What it really comes down to here is you want to think of flipping as a business. You already have a preconceived idea of how much money you'd like to earn. With this in mind, it's up to you to make those earnings a reality.

At the same time, flipping is also an investment. As such, you're bound to encounter risks along the way. It's up to you to decide, ahead of time, how much profit you need to make to make the risks worthwhile. Of course, you can lower your risk by using cash instead of depending on financing. You should also only buy a house you could rent if the market were to quickly turn soft. For instance, don't flip a pool house because if you can't sell it you don't want to rent this type of house. Also, remember pool houses come with high insurance costs.

Since you don't want to see your costs pile up, it's important you're ready to start working on your flip immediately after closing. This means buying all your materials and scheduling your contractors for that day because you want to make sure you rehab your flip as fast as possible. Each day your property remains unsold eats up your profit in the form of taxes, insurance, utilities, and maintenance.

Conclusion

Thank you again for buying this book! I hope this book helped you to start your flipping business. While there are so many things involved in a profitable flip, you now have the tools to make yours happen. The next step is to go ahead and buy your first property.

This is an exciting time for you! Don't get overwhelmed with the various steps involved in your first flip. Remember! Everything you need is right here in this book, so when you start feeling overwhelmed, go back and read through things again.

Finally, please consider check out our Amazon Author Page at https://www.amazon.com/-/e/B01LYIFPLO

Here you will find all you need to know about Rental Property Investing, Real Estate Sales, Real Estate Investing, REITs, Credit Score Repair, and even Tiny House Living if that's something you fancy!! If you check out our Real Estate Library, you are guaranteed to profit from Real Estate Investing and turn this into a lucrative income stream for the rest of your life. Don't miss out!!

Last but certainly not least, if you found this book useful in anyway, a review on Amazon is always appreciated! You can write a review on our book's page which can be accessed through this link:

https://www.amazon.com/Flipping-Houses-Comprehensive-Beginners-Properties-ebook/dp/B01MQCR30P/

Thank You and Best of Luck!!

Flipping Houses

The Cardinal Rules for Success

Introduction

I want to thank you and congratulate you for purchasing the book *Flipping Houses: The Cardinal Rules for Success*. This book is a continuation of my previous book- *Flipping Houses: Comprehensive Beginners Guide for Newbies*- and it will take you beyond the basic knowledge that you may already have regarding the topic of flipping houses. It will reveal to you how you can garner the greatest possibility for success within the house flipping market by providing you with specific strategies on how to accomplish this large and sometimes overwhelming goal. This book should not be regarded as a beginner's guide; rather, it should be perceived as being able to provide a deeper conversation. Who knows, when you're finished reading this book you may even be able to use it as an informal mentor that can guide you during each step of the flipping house process.

This book contains proven steps and strategies on how to become a truly reputable and professional housing reseller. After learning the various techniques that are presented in this book, we guarantee that implementing this knowledge will result in larger profit margins and will provide ease for you throughout the overall planning process. With this book as your guide, you'll better understand the nuances that exist within the flipping housing market. This type of information can prove to be invaluable when you are confronted with tough choices that need decisions quickly. Of course, as an aspiring real estate investor you should constantly be challenging yourself to be continuously educated. In this way, it's safe to say that you've made a fantastic purchase.

Here's an inescapable fact: you will need to have some sort of a working knowledge base about flipping houses and a commitment to earning money on your terms in order to fully benefit from the contents of this book. Maybe you've been researching techniques on how to flip houses but you're finding that internet articles don't tell the full story. Or maybe you've already flipped a few houses, but you're not seeing the profits you were hoping for. Regardless of which aspect of the flipping housing journey you're on, it's safe to say that you're likely to benefit from this book if you have your priorities and goals aligned with making money by flipping houses.

If you do not develop your knowledge of the cardinal rules to follow when flipping houses, your real estate investing endeavor is likely to flop. That means you'll spend tons of money renovating the "perfect" home for resale, only to find out that you'll never see this money again.

Additionally, the art of Flipping Houses is only one component of the multi-faceted approach that falls under the broad spectrum of Real Estate Investing. Our books tackle all these other components in detail as well. To name just a few other topics that a successful Real Estate Investor should strive to understand, we have Rental Property Investing, Real Estate Sales with details on how to embark on a career as a successful Real Estate Agent, and even a step by step guide to achieving an excellent Credit Score to get you the loan with the best rates. And for anyone interested in the Tiny House Movement, we have books on that subject as well!!

You can find books on all of these topics- AND MORE- by visiting our Amazon Author Page at the following link: https://www.amazon.com/-/e/B01LYIFPLO

While this guide to Flipping Houses will provide a detailed technical analysis of the science behind the Flip, our other books will focus much more in depth on Real Estate Investing in general. If you check out our Real Estate Library, you are guaranteed to profit from Real Estate, Rental Properties, Flipping Houses, and turn this into a lucrative income stream for the rest of your life. Don't miss out!!

It's time for you to become amazingly well versed in the art of flipping houses. Let's get started!

Chapter 1
Typical Mistakes that Newbie Flippers Make and How to Avoid Them

You've got your first flip property all picked out, and you've settled your finances with your mortgage lender and other loan organizations. Now it's time to fix this property up and get it back on the market. After that you'll be rolling in the dough in no time, right? Wrong!

Hopefully, you're not so naïve as to think that you'll easily make money through little research or little to no concern for time management. This chapter will focus on the common mistakes that newbie house flippers make, with extra emphasis on how you can avoid these mistakes. Hopefully, with the tips presented in this chapter, you'll be able to quickly elevate yourself from a beginner in the industry to someone who is competitive, money-driven, and cost effective in your decision making.

Flipping Mistake 1: Underestimating Your Budget

If there is one single cardinal rule that you should take from this book, it's to not underestimate the budget that you'll need in order to flip a property. This mistake is made so often and can be so detrimental to the overall flipping process that a discussion on how to calculate the After Repair Value (ARV) of a property has been given an entire chapter in this book. While we will go into much more depth on how to properly calculate how much a flip will cost, it's important to tally up all of the little things that you buy while you're buying and renovating your property.

Along these lines, you should consider doubling the amount of money you think you'll need as you budget for your first flip. That way, if anything goes awry, you'll have plenty of cushion as you fall.

Flipping Mistake 2: Failing to Recognize that Time is Money

In addition to underestimating exactly how much money you'll need as you begin your flipping home venture, many investors do not adequately anticipate how much time it will take to remodel a home. Sure, most of us have seen an episode of "Love It or List It" or some other show that features homeowners fixing up their properties; however, seeing something being accomplished within an hour televised window and actually taking on the process itself are two completely different things entirely. For example, consider the process of painting a room. Without being able to allot adequate time for the paint to dry and the cut ins to be appropriately done, a two-day job can end up taking a week or two.

Flipping Mistake 3: Being Stubborn About Contractors

It's pretty safe to say that at one time or another, a house flipper has thought to him or herself, "What can this contractor do that I can't?" While it's obvious that if most people took the time and made the effort to learn every aspect involved when renovating a home, he or she would be able to do so, it remains a fact that developing these skills simultaneously would take a significant amount of time. Sure, it'd be a huge money saver if you could figure out how to install a subfloor and understand the intricacies of electrical work all in a few months, but this often isn't possible. Hiring a contractor or other type of professional who can pick up the slack when a task is beyond your capabilities is sometimes a necessary evil. Of course, hiring someone to finish a job requires money, but in the end it is money well spent. When you go to flip the property, you don't want it to look like an amateur performed the work.

Flipping Mistake 4: Falling in Love with Your Property

Especially when you buy your first property, you might get excited and want to make the house exactly how you imagine it from a personal perspective. This is a serious mistake. While having large bay windows and a giant kitchen might be in the plans for your individual dream home, these shouldn't be aspects that you try to accommodate for your flipped property. Of course, adding these features might make the property sell faster when you finally put it on the market, but this value pales in comparison to the money that you'll spend while finalizing these renovations. Unless you buy an expensive property to begin with, it's likely that you won't see this money again. To avoid making this type of mistake, consider comparing how nice your property should look to those that exist around it. After you've figured out how the average property looks in the area that you're flipping, try to renovate in a way so that your property is only slightly nicer aesthetically. This way, your property will still look superior to the others, but you'll have spent less money overall.

Flipping Mistake 5: Using Your Friends as Contractors

Of course, most people want to help out their friends whenever they can. The same holds true in the real estate industry. Think about it. Most people have a friend of a friend who's a real estate agent, or a plumber, or an electrician, the list goes on. While it's certainly a better idea to hire someone when you know that the scope of construction work is beyond your individual ability, you should also shy away from hiring people simply because you want to do someone a favor.

This mistake goes hand-in-hand with doing too much of the renovation work yourself. You need to look at flipping houses as more of a business and less as a hobby or leisure activity whenever possible. Flipping a house is hard work (unless you have gobs of money lying around), and you need reputable people working for you who can get the job done at a reasonable price. You can either learn this the hard way and hire lousy people time and time again, or you can research your contractors. Find their webpages, ask around, and look for the best contractor that exists within your budget range.

Chapter 2
Repairs that Aren't Worth Your Money

While the previous chapter focused on mistakes that should definitely be avoided whenever possible as you work towards flipping a home, this chapter will provide you with even more detail in terms of avoiding properties that need specific types of repairs, either because they're simply old homes or because the previous owners were careless. By understanding the types of repairs that aren't worth your time or your money, you'll be able to begin your home buying search knowing what it is you can live with and what factors will lead you to looking elsewhere. Along with recognizing what you should avoid, we'll also gather information on how much these risk factors cost to be removed or fixed.

Top Tip 1: Avoid Homes Containing Asbestos Materials

If you've been around the real estate world for some time now, this may not be news for you, but if you're new to the flipping house market it's good to know that you should avoid homes that contain asbestos. People began using asbestos to build their houses in the early 1940s because of its ability to serve as an insulator for sound and energy such as heat. It was also revered for its fire-repellant quality. While these various uses of asbestos are positive, the problem lies in the fact that when broken apart, asbestos becomes highly dangerous to human lungs. Today, it's well known that if asbestos enters the lungs it can cause cancer and lung disease. It's not uncommon for people to walk away from buying a home that contains any asbestos at all, and as a seller who is interested in saving money, you should also avoid asbestos whenever possible.

The Cost of Removing Asbestos from a Home

Here is an average breakdown of how much asbestos removal can cost:

- **Contracted Removal:** Between $1,500 to $3,000

- **Lab Analysis of Asbestos Samples**: Between $25 to $75 per sample

- **Follow-Up Inspection of Previously Contaminated Area:** Between $200 to $400

This brings the total cost of an asbestos removal to be between $1,725 and $3,475. For these monetary reasons alone, it should be obvious that you should either demand that the seller removes any powdered forms of asbestos that exists within the home prior to your purchase, or you should walk away from the home altogether.

How to Remove Asbestos DIY

It's important to note that while asbestos can be found in building materials such as certain types of drywall, plaster, and vinyl flooring, as long as the material is intact and not decaying into a dust that can contaminate the lungs it is considered safe. If you do end up finding a home that contains harmful forms of asbestos and you are considering removing it yourself, know that this is ill-advised. If this advisory still does not deter you, the materials that you'll need include:

- A respirator mask

- Gloves

- Disposable clothing that you don't care about

- Safety goggles for eye protection

While you should make sure that your lungs and body are protected from directly coming into contact with any asbestos, you will also need to clean the asbestos-infected area with water to ensure that the particles do not contaminate the air around you. If you are removing asbestos in sheets, make sure to handle them with care. If you break the boards or sheets, the asbestos fibers are likely to break and become toxic.

Top Tip 2: Be Weary of Properties with Pools

In addition to avoiding homes containing asbestos, another rule that many house flippers swear by is avoiding properties with pools. Pools, especially if they're broken, will require costly maintenance if you're looking to refurbish them for resale. This means you will have to have a working knowledge of how to repair pool fixtures such as pumps and filtration systems. Additionally, a pool typically adds value to a home, meaning that you will be spending more money up front when you initially purchase the home. In terms of house flipping strategy, purchasing a home at a higher price does not seem like a good idea because you're inheriting more risk from the onset.

An even more financially-focused reason why you should avoid properties with pools is if you're looking to flip properties and rent them out. Regardless of whether or not you will be flipping duplexes or single unit homes, there are generally state regulations regarding pool ownership. For example, in New Jersey you must have a fence around your entire yard in order to be allowed to erect a pool within the space. Additionally, your homeowner's insurance is guaranteed to increase if you decide to maintain a pool while having tenants.

This makes sense. If something were to happen to the tenants in the pool while you weren't at the unit, the consequences could be severely detrimental to you if you did not have adequate insurance coverage. For these reasons, pools should be avoided, unless you happen to know a lot about pool maintenance and upkeep. The overall risk is too high for most investors to take this type of chance.

Top Tip 3: Avoid Homes with High Levels of Radon

The last problem that is worth avoiding is radon. With radon being found in one out of every fifteen houses in the U.S., it's worth knowing about the risks associated with it in high levels. Radon is a radioactive gas that cannot be seen, smelt, or tasted. It's dangerous because while its invisibility seems harmless, it's actually the second leading cause of cancer in the United States. Additionally, it doesn't matter if your home has just been built or if it is one hundred years old; radon can permeate the floor of your basement or living space (if you don't have a basement) through air and also aquatically.

The Cost of Radon Abatement

Depending on the severity of the radon infiltration, this type of repair can cost between $800 to $1,500. These prices might seem steep or cheap to you personally, but a more universal reality is that this type of gas can come back again and again in high levels if it's not properly treated. The possibility exists that high levels of radon will create long term problems for any tenants or future home owners that come to live in the home after you're done flipping it.

It's for these life threatening reasons that you should avoid purchasing a house where radon is prevalent. If you do end up purchasing a home that is ripe with radon gas, you should consider testing its levels every so often. It's likely too that this type of home will be harder to sell if the prospective buyer knows that radon might be an issue. If you find a home that is simply irresistible yet suffers from high levels of radon, it's highly recommended that you coerce the seller into remediating the radon instead of having to deal with this problem yourself after the deal has been closed.

Chapter 3
The Importance of an Exit Strategy

Here you have spent so much time thinking about how you should go about entering the flipping housing market that there's a chance that you forgot to think about how you will finalize your deal and make your profit. As you progress through the details of confirming your mortgage loans, getting the proper home inspections done, and beginning the repairs that are needed for your property, it can sometimes to be easy to get lost in the shuffle. That's why it's important to plan your exit strategy ahead of time, so that your actions up until the exiting point can directly relate to the overall goals that you have for your flipped property. Here we will look at strategies that are important when deciding which exit strategy to use for a particular house that you've bought.

What is an Exit Strategy?

Before we dive into the nitty gritty of what exactly to do and think about as you plan your exit strategy, it's important to first understand what an exit strategy is. The need for an exit strategy would not exist if every sale that a house flipper participated in ended smoothly. Because of the high risk that investors take responsibility of when they decide to flip a home, it's obvious that there are often both winners and losers within this highly competitive and volatile marketplace.

This being the case, the most succinct definition of an exit strategy involves planning ahead of time how you will remove yourself from a flipping housing situation if and when the time comes when it is no longer profitable or safe for you to hold onto your investment. Every house flipper obviously hopes that their house will reveal itself to be maximally profitable, but this does not always happen. This is why an exit strategy is beyond critical. It's essential to your planning process.

The Most Important Aspect of an Exit Strategy

While this chapter will focus on different types of exit strategies that can exist for a flipped house, the most important factor to remember in general is to give yourself as many options as possible. Imagine if you were to only develop one exit strategy for a house that you're going to flip, because you think that the house is a shoe in. The day finally comes. You stick the "For Sale" sign on the lawn and wait for the offers to start rolling in; however, they never do. You're optimistic and continue to be patient, hoping that someone will make you the offer of your dreams. Unfortunately, you miscalculated somewhere along the way. Your house just won't sell at the price you intended, and now you're stuck with a vacant property. If you had given yourself more than one exit strategy, you'd be in a better overall position. Regardless of the specific exit strategies that we'll focus on in this chapter, remembering that you need more than one exit strategy is the most important lesson of this chapter.

Exit Strategy Option 1: Lower Your Price

If you're optimistic and hopeful, it might be hard to eventually make the decision to lower your asking price after you've put your flipped house on the market; however, asking for less money might be the most preferable option so that even greater amounts of money won't be lost. Once you've made the decision to lower your asking price, the next question that you have to answer is how much should you lower the asking price by? There are two key factors that can help you come to a sound conclusion:

1. **Your Breakeven Price:** Your breakeven price is the price that you must sell your property for in order to not gain or lose any money. Of course, most investors want to see a profit from the time and money that they've spent flipping the house, but if you are losing money waiting to fill a property vacancy, your business can suffer potentially disastrous and obliterating consequences. Knowing your breakeven price can lower your overall loss and make it possible to know exactly by how much you can lower your price.

2. **Expiration Date on Your Loan:** As you make the decision to lower the asking price on your flipped property, it's also good to know when your loan will expire or reach its maturation point. If you don't have any debt to pay off good for you, but most house flippers will have to be cognizant of how much money is owed against the property that is not selling. Being aware of this date, along with knowing your breakeven price will help you to make smart and informed decisions if the time comes when you need to lower your asking price.

Exit Strategy Option 2: Consider a Lease Option

Perhaps your flipped house isn't selling the way that you'd hoped, but you have found one prospective buyer who currently finds him or herself in a unique situation. He or she is going through financial hardship. For example, maybe their credit needs repairing but they have the funds available to buy the place from you. You can give them the option to put a down payment on the house, and then buy the place from you at a later time. A lease option is arguably more profitable than renting because in addition to a down payment and monthly rent, you can also charge a lease fee.

Exit Strategy Option 3: You Play Landlord

If you can't find someone with the capital to participate in a lease option and you are hesitant to lower your asking price, your best bet would be to rent out your property. While it's obvious that it still might be difficult to rent out the property if it's a single unit home, everyone's living situation is unique and you might be able to find someone or a family who is interested in renting a single family home. Keep in mind, while this exit strategy is potentially profitable, you will still have responsibilities as a landlord if you choose this route. If you truly want to remove yourself from the daily functions of the home, consider hiring a property manager. Also consider checking out my book – *Rental Property Millionaire: Comprehensive Beginner's Guide for Newbies*- prior to becoming a landlord.

Chapter 4:
How to Calculate Your ARV like a Pro

The ARV, or After Repair Value, of an investment property is perhaps the most important number you will have to calculate as a real estate investor. Not only is it instrumental in determining which property you will choose to flip, it also helps resolve how much you can expect your profit to be when all is said and done. The ARV is the projected value of a house once all repairs and renovations have been completed. There are several factors to consider when calculating and determining whether or not the ARV is worth your investment. You will likely need some help from a licensed real estate agent to obtain the most accurate ARV possible, but it can be broken down to a fairly simple science that you should be able to apply to all of your resale endeavors if you want to become a lucrative real estate investor.

Step 1: Comparable Property Sales

You won't get a very accurate estimate of your subject property's value without taking a good look at the local housing market. It behooves you to research other properties that are as similar as possible to what yours will be after the full renovation (hereby referred to as "comps"), and take note of what these houses have sold for. There are many online resources available to the potential buyer to accomplish this, such as Zillow and Realtor.com. The most detailed and accurate source of information, however, will undoubtedly be the multiple listing service (or MLS), which you will most likely need to access through a licensed agent. The goal is to make a list of at least three different comps to help evaluate your subject property.

Before you gather a list of comps it helps to adequately define what a true comp is. First of all, you want to look exclusively at *sold* properties, not those that are currently for sale. This is a common mistake for beginner real estate investors. You can never assume that the asking price of a house is its official value, since most properties end up selling for less; sometimes a lot less. After all, if the asking price was the true value, the house wouldn't still be for sale. Second, you want to investigate houses that match what your subject property *will* become, not those that match its current state. When the dust settles on the renovation the house should be more valuable than when it was purchased, and that is the number we really want to find out.

The most important criteria for judging an adequate comp are the following:

1. **Date of Sale** - Narrow your search down to houses that have sold within the last six months, perhaps even three if you're looking in a particularly active market.

2. **Location** - Rule of thumb is to look within a half-mile radius, but this can vary depending on the environment. In a densely populated city, for instance, real estate values might increase dramatically from street to street.

3. **Age**

4. **Style** - More traditional styles tend to sell for less than more modern homes

5. **Size** - Ideally, your comps should fall within 10% of the finished square footage, and have the same number of bedrooms and bathrooms

6. **Condition** - Is the house move-in-ready? Does it require extensive repairs? When was the last update? It's also very important to note that regardless of the condition, a distressed sale (foreclosure or short-sale, for example) is NOT a comparable property. This is another pitfall that many new flippers encounter when calculating their ARV.

Step 2: Adjusting the Values of Your Comps

Once you have your list of comps, it's time to adjust those resale values to account for all the features your subject property will eventually have. You want to add or subtract value from the sale price to reflect what the comp would have sold for if it was equivalent to your subject property in every way possible. For example, say comp #1 sold at $200,000 with three bedrooms and 1.5 bathrooms. Your subject property will have three bedrooms and two bathrooms.

Assuming that is the only differentiating factor between the two houses, the comp would have sold for more than $200,000 since two full baths is more valuable than 1.5. Let's say a full-bath is worth 1.5% more on the sale price than a half-bath (please note that this percentage is highly dependent on the market and it's recommended to consult a real estate professional for these types of estimates). This means the comp would have sold for $203,000 if it matched your subject property's features.

This type of adjustment should be made for all of your comps. Consider all of the criteria you used when establishing your comps in the beginning; finished square footage, age, condition, etc.; as well as things like the amount of garage storage space, fireplaces, updated utility systems, and so on. Consult a professional when necessary to help you find the relative values of these features. You should end up with a spreadsheet or table to help you compare all of these adjusted sale prices.

Step 3: Evaluating the Subject Property

Once you've established the adjusted values of all your comps, you can make a projection of your subject property's worth. This should match the lowest adjusted comp value, or a conservative average of all of them. For example, say we have a list of three comps; the adjusted sale prices are $203,000, $210,000, and $205,550 respectively. From here, we can assume the subject property is worth somewhere between $203,000 and $210,000. As we've discussed, it's recommended to be as conservative as possible, and assume the property is worth the lowest of the three. However, you can reasonably take the average ($206,183) and assume your subject property is worth that price. This, at last, is your After Repair Value; your ARV.

Now, why does this number matter so much? First of all, an established cardinal rule for real estate investing is to not spend more than 70% of your ARV on purchasing and renovating your flip. In the example above, if our ARV is $206,183, we should strive to spend $144,328 or less on buying and rehabbing the subject property. Let's say the asking price on the subject property is $135,500; that only leaves us with $8,828 to renovate the house with. If we plan on an extensive rehab, this may not be the property we want to end up with. Concordantly, this 70% rule in conjunction with the ARV tells you how much you can expect to profit from the flip. In this case, $61,855 should be left over from the sale. Make the necessary adjustments for taxes, broker fees, financing costs, etc. to find your bottom line.

Chapter 5
The Value of a Team Effort

Many new real estate investors are disillusioned by the notion that they need to handle every aspect of the process themselves, from the initial market research to screwing in the last lightbulb. This is simply not true. Yes, substituting your own time and labor for somebody else's is usually to your financial advantage. However, this is a highly specialized market, with many variables and moving parts, and it can be too easy to stretch yourself too thin. Not only can this be a sizable burden to your well-being, it can also lead to costly mistakes that could have been avoided if you had consulted a professional. Flipping a property should be a team effort, and you will benefit in the growth of your investment business by having a group-oriented mentality. The following is an analysis of the key members of an ideal house-flipping team.

Lenders

It should be well-established by now that real estate investing is a very costly process. This is especially true when first starting out, and capital is low. Securing a reliable source of money is paramount to getting your business up and running. As was discussed in the beginner's guide, this can come from a wide range of sources including large mortgage brokers and private investors. Where the money comes from will depend largely on your financial standing before diving into the real estate game, but what's important for the purpose of our discussion here is the development of a solid relationship with your lender, or lenders.

Establishing trust and accountability with your lenders is crucial to your success. They are expecting you to be able to back up their investment in you, after all. This is especially true of private investors who you may know on a personal level. Knowing *who* the person is on the other side of the deal will really help alleviate the stress and anxiety that often comes with these types of interactions. It also helps to establish a solid working relationship with someone who you may choose to approach for future investment opportunities. These relationships can turn into long-term partnerships that create more opportunities for you, as well.

Realtor

Finding a good real estate agent can significantly help secure the best deals and simplify much of the research involved with finding lucrative investment opportunities. They will also be instrumental in making sure your house gets sold at a profitable value. You should try to find a realtor that has experience dealing with flipping houses. If your intentions are clear from the start, they will be better suited to help you reach your goals. It's also important to hire one that is amenable to how you like to do business. You want to establish a relationship with a realtor that you can rely on long-term to maximize the benefit to both parties for all future endeavors.

It's not uncommon to work with multiple agents that specialize in different markets. As you progress in your real estate investment business, it may be to your advantage to find realtors that excel in short-sales and bank foreclosures. As you become more experienced and confident in your flipping endeavors, these people will become extremely helpful in finding the best deals on purchasing distressed properties.

Certified Public Accountant

Much like finding the right accountant for your personal taxes, hiring the right CPA for your real estate investment business is important to save you money and stress. It's essential to find one who knows the national and local property tax code forward and backward. One who is experienced with flipping houses and really understands how to interpret real estate accounting laws may be hard to come across, but it is well worth your time and effort. A good CPA will do their best to legally keep your taxes low, as well as offer their counsel on the growth and structure of your business; from a financial and legal perspective.

General Contractor

Unless you are a well-accomplished builder or contractor yourself, you will need to rely on a competent GC for the bulk of your renovation projects. Since most of the surprises come during the renovation, this could potentially be the most tumultuous relationship among your entire house-flipping team. It's important, then, that you establish a good working relationship with one that is understanding of your goals and easy to get along with if and when things get dicey. You should look for one who is as detail-oriented as possible, and will give you the most accurate estimates they can.

It's very common to work with multiple different GC's, and encouraged since you want as diversified an expertise as you can get. The general contractor is also your main connection to all the subcontractors who will be working on various specialized aspects of the project. As such, the lines of communication should be as open and responsive as possible. It helps to have a team of contractors that have worked with each other in the past. If any issues arise that were not anticipated in the initial scope of work, a team of contractors that are familiar and friendly with each other will be more flexible as a unit and be able to adapt to the changing flow of work more easily.

The ideal general contractor should also be someone who you can be firm with without creating friction in the relationship that affects the project. You must be able to hold them accountable for the budgets and the timeframes that were agreed upon before the work starts. Likewise, the GC is responsible for keeping all of the subcontractors in line to get the work done in a timely and economical manner. Establishing your goals and enforcing a chain-of-command right from the start will help minimize any potential delays.

While it's important to create a strong team to set yourself up for success, it's very rare to find the perfect candidates during your first time. Your first experiences with flipping houses will help you develop criteria for picking the right people for the long-term. Expect things to not move as efficiently as possible on your first go-around. The most important thing, however, is to realize that you should never have to settle with someone who doesn't work to the best of their abilities to help you achieve your goals. You can afford to shop around for good help.

Chapter 6
Ways to Keep Renovation Costs Low

When it's time to get down to the actual meat-and-potatoes of flipping a house, the physical rehab, it's important to be as meticulously prepared as possible. It's also worth noting that when looking at the grand scheme of a project, every little thing adds up, and you should be considering every small detail in your plan to maximize your profit. But like you've been warned before, it's very easy to end up dishing out more than you expected to pay. This is the aspect of house flipping that takes the hardest experience to really become adept at. Especially for your first project, factor in a 10-20% cushion to your budget plan to cover any surprises or oversights that may arise. No matter how prepared you may be, there is always going to be the risk of unforeseen costs. However, there are lots of little tips and tricks to help you keep those renovation costs as small as possible.

Efficiency of Space

While it may be glamorous to add square footage to the kitchen by building a large addition, sometimes a perceived lack of space can be remedied by diversifying the space that's given. Rather than build up/out, build within by maximizing usable surface areas. Replace large shelves with cabinets that contain pull-out drawers, dividers, or lazy Susans. Instead of expanding the kitchen out into the yard, sometimes replacing half of a wall for a breakfast bar is all you need. Maximizing the amount of horizontal planes wherever you can will eliminate the need for more square footage. Upgraded cabinetry can be expensive, sure, but it will cost you a fraction of what you could have spent on a large addition.

Limit the Amount of Lighting Fixtures

You want to cut down on installing recessed lighting whenever possible. The fixtures themselves can be costly enough, but there's also a lot of labor in cutting out individual holes and insulating them. A single overhead fixture can even produce more wattage than a handful of recessed lightbulbs, and cost you several hundred dollars less. Maximizing the effect of natural light can also go a long way. You'd be surprised how much proper drapery can let in ample light. A new trend in modern homes is the use of "sun tubes" to bring in sunlight to windowless areas. These tubes are installed between roof rafters and reflect the sunlight down into the living space without the need to cut out large expanses of the exterior. These tubes can easily save you a thousand dollars or more over adding a double-paned window where there wasn't one previously. The color palette of the interior also has an understated effect on the amount of illumination a room can receive. Lighter paints and fabrics are better at reflecting natural light and can help you cut down on the cost of installing more light fixtures.

Use Recycled Materials

You can drastically cut down your renovation costs by using recycled or lightly used building materials. One terrific resource is a Habitat for Humanity ReStore. These places provide repurposed materials and fixtures for roughly 50% of what you would pay at a Home Depot or Lowe's. You would be surprised at how much can be collected from these stores. Prehung doors, skylights and windows, insulation, and flooring are just a few things that can be found here.

You can also inquire if your subcontractors have any materials left over from previous jobs that can be repurposed for your project. Especially with things like flooring, sheetrock, and lumber, it's certainly worth investigating. Even if the floorboards from a previous project don't exactly match what you're looking for, the cost of whatever refinishing or planing needs to be done will pale in comparison to what brand new boards will cost you. You can also purchase some of your materials at a building supply auction. There are loads to be found at these events: misordered custom pieces, overstock supplies, and lightly damaged goods, to name a few. A single wooden cabinet can cost you hundreds of dollars from a home improvement store, but you could walk away from an auction with that same cabinet for only a few dollars.

Sweat Equity

By far the best way to save money on the renovation is to do the work yourself. This doesn't necessarily mean you have to be an experienced builder who can tackle the whole project. Any way in which you can cut down the labor cost is hugely beneficial. A common method many real estate investors employ is handling the demolition themselves. You don't need nearly as much expertise to dear town as you do to build up, and even though the cost of demolition is minor compared to rebuilding, it will make a noticeable dent in your budget. You can also handle some or all of the finish work yourself, like painting or installing minor fixtures or appliances once the bones are in place. Sweat equity can be as simple as delivering your own supplies. If you have access to a pickup truck or a trailer, you can save up to hundreds on the material delivery fees that come with sheet goods like drywall and plywood.

Don't Move the Sink or Toilet

Though it may seem like an odd addition to this list, it costs a lot more than you may think to relocate plumbing fixtures. Rerouting pipes and tinkering with water flow can easily become the largest part of your plumbing rehab price. Try to leave the sinks and toilets where they are when conceiving your new plan.

Develop a Plan Early and Stick to It

There's no greater enemy to renovation costs than "might as well's" and "while you're at it" statements. You want to have as fully thought-out a plan as possible before you start doing any of the demolition. Know what types of fixtures and appliances you want, and how much they will cost beforehand. You can never be too specific. A common mistake is to rely on the subcontractor's allowance without making sure the two of you are in total agreement on what is to be put in. Allowances are almost always too low, and you don't want to get slapped with a higher estimate when the subcontractor thought you wanted a slightly different material installed.

It helps tremendously to keep open lines of communication amongst your network of contractors. Unexpected expenses and delays happen quite often, and can easily set back further work that was scheduled down the line, which will inevitably cost you more time and money. It is recommended to schedule a meeting with your GC and all of the subcontractors who will be working on the project before any of the demolition has begun. Make sure everybody understands the budget and timeline you have set. It helps if all of the contractors have each others' contact info so they can communicate independently without having to go through you or the GC to relay any messages to the rest of the team. If a problem arises, make sure *everybody* is made aware of it before proceeding with another part of the renovation. This will help your team of contractors work as a unit and ensure the work gets done as smoothly as possible.

Consider Imitations

There a several imitation building materials that should be looked at when planning your renovation. Lyptus wood, for example, is a eucalyptus hybrid that captures the aesthetic and feel of natural mahogany hardwood, for a fraction of the price. Another example is Texturglas wall coverings, which are made of fiberglass filaments, and are much cheaper alternatives to fully patching and painting damaged walls.

It is Not Your Dream Home

Many new real estate investors fall into the trap of projecting what *they* would want in their living space without considering the costs that accompany this vision. It's important to remind yourself that you are doing this for profit above all else, and what you find desirable in a new home may not be the same as what a potential buyer does. You should consider cheaper alternatives to what you might envision in your ideal home. You may love the look of a giant bay window in the living room, but if that is going to add thousands of dollars to your budget when you can easily keep the existing ones or just add a single new window, it's advised to go with the latter. Unless the buyer is a professional chef, they likely won't need a commercial-standard range. Glass shower doors are another unnecessary expense. These most likely will need to be custom-fitted and traditional shower curtains are a negligible expense.

Minimizing your renovation cost is a very nuanced process, and will likely take some trial-and-error in developing a sound system. The suggestions outlined above are but a starting outline for ways you can look to save. The important thing to remember is that no amount of savings is too minute; it all adds up to sizable dollars in the end.

Conclusion

Thank you again for purchasing this book!

I hope this book was able to help you to better understand how you can maximize the cash that exists within the investment strategy of flipping properties. If you follow the tips that are presented in this book, it's safe to say that you'll be making smarter decisions for yourself and for your business. These strategies, when utilized properly, can take your earnings to the next level. You'll feel more comfortable within the industry as a whole, and you'll be able to implement your processes faster. Remember, time is money! Investing in your education will expand your opportunities in ways that you may have never thought possible.

The next step is to begin calculating the After Repair Value on properties that seem like they would make sound investments. If you've already done this, consider looking at factors within the specific market that you're interested in entering and in which you wish to purchase your property. Lastly, don't undervalue the importance of building a top notch team who can support your flipping efforts. You're not expected to be the best at every aspect of house flipping, but you are expected to find different people who collectively are!

Finally, if you enjoyed this book please consider check out our Amazon Author Page at https://www.amazon.com/-/e/B01LYIFPLO

Here you will find all you need to know about Rental Property Investing, Real Estate Sales, Real Estate Investing, REITs, Credit Score Repair, and even Tiny House Living if that's something you fancy!! If you check out our Real Estate Library, you are guaranteed to profit from Real Estate

Investing and turn this into a lucrative income stream for the rest of your life. Don't miss out!!

Last but certainly not least, if you found this book useful in anyway, a review on Amazon is always appreciated! You can write a review on our book's page which can be accessed through this link:

https://www.amazon.com/Flipping-Houses-Comprehensive-Beginners-Properties-ebook/dp/B01MQCR30P/

Thank you and good luck!

Made in the USA
Columbia, SC
25 October 2022

70026536R00052